FREE DVD

MW01137032

Essential Test Tips DVD from Trivium Test Prep

Dear Customer,

Thank you for purchasing from Cirrus Test Prep! Whether you're looking to join the military, get into college, or advance your career, we're honored to be a part of your journey.

To show our appreciation (and to help you relieve a little of that test-prep stress), we're offering a **FREE *Praxis Essential Test Tips DVD**** by Cirrus Test Prep. Our DVD includes 35 test preparation strategies that will help keep you calm and collected before and during your big exam. All we ask is that you email us your feedback and describe your experience with our product. Amazing, awful, or just so-so: we want to hear what you have to say!

To receive your **FREE *Praxis Essential Test Tips DVD***, please email us at 5star@cirrustestprep.com. Include "Free 5 Star" in the subject line and the following information in your email:

1. The title of the product you purchased.
2. Your rating from 1 – 5 (with 5 being the best).
3. Your feedback about the product, including how our materials helped you meet your goals and ways in which we can improve our products.
4. Your full name and shipping address so we can send your **FREE *Praxis Essential Test Tips DVD***.

If you have any questions or concerns please feel free to contact us directly at 5star@cirrustestprep.com. Thank you, and good luck with your studies!

* Please note that the free DVD is <u>not included</u> with this book. To receive the free DVD, please follow the instructions above.

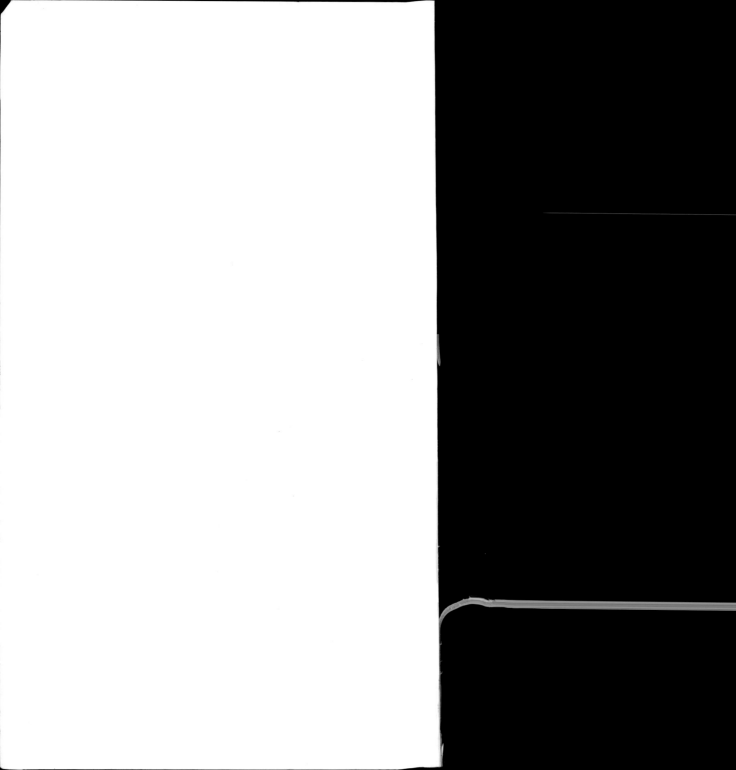

Praxis II Elementary Education Multiple Subjects 5001 Flash Cards

OVER 800 PRAXIS ELEMENTARY EDUCATION FLASH CARDS FOR TEST PREP REVIEW

Table of Contents

Introduction

Congratulations on choosing to take the Praxis Elementary Education: Multiple Subjects (5001) exam! By purchasing this book, you've taken the first step toward becoming an elementary educator.

WHAT IS THE PRAXIS?

Praxis Series tests are a part of teaching licensure in approximately forty states. Each state uses the tests and scores in different ways, so be sure to check the certification requirements in your state by going to www.ets.org/praxis/states. There, you will find information detailing the role of the Praxis tests in determining teaching certification in your state, what scores are required, and how to transfer Praxis scores from one state to another.

WHAT'S ON THE PRAXIS?

The content in this guide will prepare you for the Praxis Elementary Education: Multiple Subjects (5001) exam. This test uses multiple-choice and numeric-entry questions to assess whether you possess the knowledge and skills necessary to become an elementary educator. The exam consists of four subtests that each assess your subject knowledge in a different area. Each subtest has a different time limit and number of questions; the approximate number of questions for each subtopic is given below. Altogether, the exam is four hours and fifteen minutes long.

Praxis 5001 Elementary Education

Section	Questions per Section	Concepts	Percent of Test	Number of Questions
Reading/ Language Arts	80	Reading	47%	38
		Writing, Speaking, and Listening	52%	42
Mathe-matics	50	Numbers and Operations	40%	20
		Algebraic Thinking	30%	15
		Geometry and Measurement, Data, Statistics, and Probability	30%	15
Social Studies	55	United States History, Government, and Citizenship	45%	25
		Geography, Anthropology, and Sociology	30%	16
		World History and Economics	25%	14
Science	50	Earth Science	32%	16
		Life Science	34%	17
		Physical Science	34%	17
Total			4.25 hours	235

You will answer approximately eighty multiple-choice questions on reading and language arts. Questions in this section will assess your own reading comprehension and vocabulary usage as well as your understanding of teaching strategies that reinforce vocabulary and language development. The foundations of reading and the use of language in writing will be assessed. You'll need to know the purposes and characteristics of effective listening and communication; likewise, you should understand the barriers that hinder interpersonal exchange.

You will answer approximately fifty multiple-choice questions on mathematics. The test will cover mathematical processes, number sense and numeration, algebraic concepts, informal geometry and measurement, and data organization and interpretation. A scientific calculator will be provided for you on this portion of the test.

You will answer approximately fifty-five multiple-choice questions on social studies. The social studies section is interdisciplinary; it will test your ability to understand relationships among fields in social studies. These fields include geography, anthropology, sociology, world and US history, government/civics/democracy, economics, and social studies as inquiry. You'll need knowledge of all of these subjects in order to answer the questions correctly.

You will answer approximately fifty multiple-choice questions on science. This section assesses your knowledge of scientific fundamentals in a wide spectrum of the sciences, including earth, life, and physical sciences, science in personal and social perspectives, and science as inquiry. Questions will explore the structure of systems, such as matter, living systems, and earth systems. Be sure to familiarize yourself with the unifying processes of science and science as a process and human endeavor.

How is the Praxis Scored?

The questions are equally weighted. Keep in mind that some multiple-choice questions are experimental questions for the purpose of the Praxis test writers and will not count toward your overall score. However, since those questions are not indicated on the test, you must respond to every question. There is no penalty for guessing on Praxis tests, so be sure to eliminate answer choices and answer every question. If you still do not know the answer, guess; you may get it right!

Your score report will be available on your Praxis account for one year, but you can also opt for a paper report. The score report includes your score and the passing score for the states you identified as score recipients. Your score will be available immediately after the test.

How is the Praxis Administered?

The Praxis Series tests are available at testing centers across the nation. To find a testing center near you, go to http://www.ets.org/praxis/register. At this site, you can create a Praxis account, check testing dates, register for a test, or find instructions for registering via mail or phone. The Praxis Elementary Education: Multiple Subjects (5001) exam is administered as a computerized test. The Praxis website allows you to take a practice test to acclimate yourself to the computerized format.

On the day of your test, be sure to bring your admission ticket (which is provided when you register) and photo ID. The testing facility will provide pencils and erasers and an area outside of the testing room to store your personal belongings. You are allowed no personal effects in the testing area. Cell phones and other electronic, photographic, recording, or listening devices are not permitted in the testing center at all, and bringing those items may be cause for dismissal, forfeiture of your testing fees, and cancellation of your scores. For details on what is and is not permitted at your testing center, refer to http://www.ets.org/praxis/test_day/bring.

ABOUT CIRRUS TEST PREP

Cirrus Test Prep study guides are designed by current and former educators and are tailored to meet your needs as an incoming educator. Our guides offer all of the resources necessary to help you pass teacher certification tests across the nation.

Cirrus clouds are graceful, wispy clouds characterized by their high altitude. Just like cirrus clouds, Cirrus Test Prep's goal is to help educators "aim high" when it comes to obtaining their teacher certification and entering the classroom.

1

English and Language Arts

academic language

active listening

language used in formal settings and academic writing

listening that is focused and empathetic

adjective

advanced fluency stage of language acquisition

adverb

a word that modifies a noun or pronoun

learners demonstrate near-native ability and use complex, multiphrase and multiclause sentences to convey their ideas

a word that modifies an adjective, adverb, verb, phrase, or clause

affixes

analyzing text organization

audience

added to words or roots to change their meanings; include prefixes (added to the beginning of a word or root) and suffixes (added to the end of a word or root)

analyzing how a text is organized in order to better comprehend an author's purpose for writing

the reader/readers

central idea

character analysis

citations

the basic underlying idea of informational text

understanding the role of a character in a story via the character's actions, traits, relationships, and personality

identification of original sources of outside information

clause

complex sentence

compound sentence

a group of words with both a subject and a predicate

a sentence made up of an independent clause and one or more dependent clauses

a sentence made up of two independent clauses (or simple sentences)

compound-complex sentence

conjunction

connotation

a sentence that has two or more independent clauses and one or more dependent clauses

joins words into phrases, clauses, and sentences

the intended meaning of a word beyond its literal meaning

conversational language

credibility

denotation

familiar and informal language

proof of the reliability of a source

the literal meaning of a word

descriptive writing

dialect

**early production stage of
language acquisition**

a writing style that emphasizes the production of imagery using words and figurative language that appeal to the reader's five senses

language that is particular to a geographical location or consolidated social group

learners produce single-word and two- to three-word phrases and can respond to questions and statements

expository writing

figurative language

first-person point of view

a writing style that explains an idea or concept or informs the reader about a topic

language that conveys images and ideas separate from the actual meanings of the words used

one character tells the story from his or her direct experience using pronouns such as *I, my, mine,* and *we*

fluency

genre

grammar

the ability to read with ease and automaticity

type of a text (e.g., poetry, drama, picture book, graphic novel, folktale, myth, fairy tale, tall tale, historical fiction, science fiction)

the way parts of speech work together in sentences and how words are grouped to make meaning such as in phrases or clauses

high frequency letter-sound
correspondences

identifying point of view

inferences

letter-sound correspondences that occur most often in the English language

using genre and pronoun clues to identify who is telling a story to best form accurate conclusions about the events of the story

conclusions about what an author suggests in a text based on context clues

interjection

intermediate fluency stage of
language acquisition

letter-sound correspondence

a word that expresses emotion

learners are able to speak in more complex sentences and catch and correct many of their errors

the relationship between the spoken sounds in words and the printed letters that correspond to those sounds

levels of language proficiency

literal

mechanics

L1) entering, L2) beginning, L3) developing, L4) expanding, and L5) bridging

the most basic or exact meaning of a word

the conventions of print that are not necessary in spoken language, such as punctuation, capitalization, and indentation (spelling is a component of mechanics but is treated as a separate category in elementary school)

meter

misplaced modifier

modifiers

the basic rhythmic structure of the lines or verses in poetry

a modifier that causes confusion because it does not modify its intended word or phrase

words or phrases that change the meanings of or add details to other words or phrases in a sentence

moral

morphemes

narrative poems

the lesson the author intends to teach the reader in a literary text

the smallest units of language that contain meaning

poems that tell stories

narrative writing

noun

onset

a writing style that tells a personal or fictional story that entertains the reader

a person, place, thing, or idea

the beginning consonant or consonant blend of a syllable

paraphrasing

persuasive writing

phoneme

briefly restating information in one's own words

a writing style that convinces, or persuades, a reader to subscribe to the author's opinion or point of view (often used for speeches and advertisements)

each small unit of sound in a language

phoneme blending

phoneme deletion

phoneme segmentation

combining phonemes to make a word

removing phonemes from words to make new words

separating phonemes in words

phoneme substitution

phonemic awareness

phonics

replacing phonemes in words to make new words

a type of phonological awareness; an understanding of how phonemes form a language by creating differences in the meanings of words

the study of the relationship between the spoken sounds in words and the printed letters that correspond to those sounds

phrase

phonological awareness

plagiarism

a group of words with either a subject or a predicate

an understanding of how sounds, syllables, words, and word parts can be orally manipulated to break apart words, make new words, and create rhymes

intentionally copying and taking credit for another person's work

plot development

preposition

preproduction stage of
language acquisition

the exposition, rising action, problem/climax, falling action, and resolution

describes relationships in time and space

the silent period; learners refrain from speaking but will listen, may copy words down, and can respond to visual cues

primary sources

pronoun

prosody

original materials representative of an event, experience, place, or time period

a word that replaces a noun

the range of vocal expressions a reader uses when reading aloud, including rhythm, intonation, and stress patterns

punctuation

qualitative measures

quantitative measures

periods, commas, question marks, exclamation marks, and other markings that divide text or help a reader know when to change pace or read with inflection

contributors to text leveling that include analysis of text elements such as structure, language clarity, and knowledge demands

contributors to text leveling that include readability scores determined by computer algorithms that evaluate text elements such as word frequency and sentence length

reader and task considerations

reading accuracy

reading rate

matching texts to particular students, classes, and/or tasks based on their inherent needs as determined by the professional judgment of educators

the ability to recognize or decode words correctly

the speed and fluidity with which a reader can read

register

reliable sources

rhyme scheme

particular styles of language determined by purpose, audience, and social context

trustworthy materials that come from experts in the field of study

rhyme pattern in a poem; may be represented as letters (e.g., *abab*, *aabb*, *aabba*)

rime

roots

second-person point of view

a syllable's vowel and its remaining consonants (not including the onset)

the basis of many words in the English language, typically derived from Latin or Greek

a narrative perspective from an external "you," whether that be the reader or unknown other

secondary sources

setting

sight words

sources that inform about events, experiences, places, or time periods using primary sources but that were not directly involved in the event in any way

where a story takes place

words that are repeated most often in text

silent period

simple sentence

speech emergence stage of language acquisition

the preproduction stage of language acquisition

a sentence that contains a subject, a verb, and a completed thought

learners can chunk simple words and phrases into sentences that may or may not be grammatically correct and can understand simple readings when reinforced by graphics or pictures

stages of language acquisition

structural analysis

summarization

preproduction, early production, speech emergence, intermediate fluency, and advanced fluency

an analysis of the roots and affixes of words

distilling and condensing a text into its main idea and key details by identifying story elements

syllables

syntax

text features

phonological units composed of onsets and rimes that can be blended, substituted, segmented, and deleted like phonemes

the grammatical formations and patterns of sentences

supplemental information outside of the main text such as chapter headings, titles, sidebars (boxes of explanatory or additional information set aside from main text) and hyperlinks

text leveling

text structure

theme

complexity of text as determined by quantitative measures, qualitative measures, and reader and task considerations

organizational structures like cause and effect, problem and solution, sequence of events or steps-in-a-process, compare and contrast, and description

the basic idea that the author wants to convey in a literary text

third-person limited omniscient point of view

third-person objective point of view

third-person omniscient point of view

a narrative perspective in which a detached narrator tells the story from one character's point of view, including that character's internal thoughts and feelings

a narrative perspective in which a detached narrator relates the actions and dialogue of the story, but not the thoughts or feelings of any characters

a narrative perspective in which a detached and all-knowing narrator tells the story from the point of view of all of the characters, including all of their thoughts and feelings

tone

unreliable sources

usage

the attitude of a text

untrustworthy materials from a person or institution that does not have the educational background, expertise, or evidence of legitimate sources to support a claim

common rules for how language is used under certain conditions or within particular styles

verb

writing styles

a word that expresses action or being

specific types of writing that convey the author's purpose for writing—to explain, to entertain, to describe, or to persuade

Mathematics

acute

acute triangle

angle between 0 and 90 degrees

has three acute angles

addition

algebraic expressions

algorithms

the process of combining two or more numbers

contain numbers, variables, and a mathematical operation

a set of steps to follow when solving a problem

angles

arc

area

a shape formed by two rays that share a common point

any portion of a circle between two points on the circle

the size of a surface measured in square units

area models (also called the box method)

arrays

associative property

a non-traditional approach to multiplication that promotes understanding of place value

a pictorial representation of a multiplication problem

in multiplication and addition, the way numbers are grouped in parentheses does not matter, $(a + b) + c = a + (b + c)$

bar graphs

base-10

binomials

a graph that uses lengths of rectangles to show data

the numbering system where each digit is worth ten times as much as the digit to the right of it

an algebraic expression with two different variables

box plots
(also called box and whisker plots)

central angle

chord

data is shown using the median and range of a data set

an angle with its vertex at the center of a circle

the part of a secant line that lies within a circle

circle

circle graphs

circumference

set of all the points in a plane that are the same distance from a fixed point

a pie chart where each "piece" demonstrates a quantity

the distance around a circle

commutative property

composite numbers

coordinate plane

in multiplication and addition, the order of the numbers on each side of the equation does not matter

$ab = ba$

a natural number greater than 1 that can be divided by at least one other number besides 1 and itself

the plane containing the x-axis and y-axis

customary units

decimals

denominator

units of measure used in the United States

any real number in the base-10 system, but often refers to numbers with digits to the right of the decimal point

the number on the bottom of a fraction

dependent variables

diameter

digits

variables with a value dependent on other variables

the largest measurement across a circle

any number 0 – 9

distributive property

dividends

division

multiplication distributes over addition, $a(b + c) = ab + ac$

a number that is being divided by another number

splitting a number into equal parts

divisors

dot plots

double bar graphs

the number by which another number is divided

a graphical display of data using dots

bar graphs that present more than one type of data

double line graphs

equations

equilateral triangle

a line graph that presents more than one type of data

algebraic expressions that use an equal sign

all three sides are equal as are all three angles

estimation

expanded form

exponent

a close prediction that involves minor calculations

breaking up a number by the value of each digit

the number written to the upper right of another number that indicates how many times that number should be multiplied by itself

factors

figures

formulas

numbers that are multiplied with each other

geometric forms made up of points, lines, or planes

mathematical relationships expressed in symbols

fraction

function

histogram

a part of a whole

a relationship between input and output

bar graph showing continuous data over time

inequalities

independent variables

integers

two mathematical quantities that are not equal to each other

values that determine the value of other variables

positive or negative whole numbers that are not fractions or decimals

inverse operations

isosceles triangle

length

an operation that reverses another operation

has two equal sides and two equal angles

the measurement of something from end to end

linear equation

line graph

line segment

an equation that results in a straight line when graphed

a graph that uses points connected by lines to show data

a part of a line that connects two points

line

mean

measures of center

a one-dimensional geometric shape that is infinitely long

the average

include mean, median, and mode

median

mental math

metric units

the number in the middle when the data set is arranged from least to greatest

math that can be done in the student's head without the use of tools

the universal units of measure

mode

model

multiples

the most frequent

a mathematical representation of the real-world

the product of two whole numbers

multiplication

natural numbers

net

repeated addition of the same number to itself

numbers used when counting; do not include zero, fractions, or decimals

the shape of a flattened three-dimensional object

numerator

obtuse

obtuse triangle

the number on top of a fraction

angle between 90 and 180 degrees

has one obtuse angle and two acute angles

one-dimensional

order of operations

ordered pair

having only length

---

work the problem in the following order
(1) parentheses and brackets, (2) exponents and square roots,
(3) multiplication and division, and (4) addition and subtraction

---

two numbers written to show the position of a point in a coordinate plane

origin

outlier

parallel lines

the point (0, 0) on a graph

a data point that is vastly different from the other data points

lines that remain the same distance apart over their entire length and never cross

percentage

perimeter

perpendicular lines

a part of a whole conveyed per 100

distance around a two-dimensional shape

lines that cross at a 90-degree angle

place value

point

polygons

the value of the location of a digit within a number

location in a coordinate plane

two-dimensional shapes that have 3 or more straight sides

prime numbers

probability

product

a natural number greater than 1 that can be divided only by 1 and itself

the likelihood that something will happen

the result of multiplying two or more numbers

quadrants

quotient

radius

the four areas created by the intersection of the *x*-axis and *y*-axis

the result of dividing one number into another

the distance from the center to any point on a circle

range

ratio

rational number

the difference between the highest number and the lowest number in a data set

a comparison of two things

a number that can be made by dividing two integers; incudes fractions and terminating or repeating decimals

ray

reasonableness

remainder

a shape that starts at one point and goes infinitely in one direction

making common sense

the number that is left over when one number does not divide evenly into another

right triangle

rounding

scalene triangle

has one right angle and two acute angles

simplifying a number to any given place value

has no equal sides or angles

scatterplot

secant

sector

a graph of plotted points that compares two data sets

a line that cuts across a circle and touches it twice

the part of a circle that is inside the rays of a central angle

similar

slope

solids

shapes that have the same angles and whose sides have a constant proportion

in a linear relationship, the change in y divided by the change in x. This is the measurement of the steepness of a line

three-dimensional objects

statistics

subtraction

surface area

the study of data

finding the difference between two numbers

the sum of the areas of all sides of a three-dimensional object

tangent

tessellations

three-dimensional

a line that touches a circle or any curve at one point

creating patterns through the tiling of polygons

having length, width, and height

trends

triangle inequality theorem

two-dimensional

two sets of data that show a pattern

that the sum of any two sides of a triangle must be greater than the third side

having length and width

unit fraction

unit rate

volume

a fraction where the numerator is 1

the ratio of two measurements in which the part is 1

the amount of space that an object occupies as measured in cubic units

whole numbers

x-axis

y-axis

counting numbers, including zero, that are not fractions or decimals

horizontal position on a graph where $y = 0$

vertical position on a graph where $x = 0$

Social Studies

abolitionism

Abraham Lincoln

the ending of slavery

first Republican president, an abolitionist elected in 1860; his election triggered Southern secession. He led the country through the Civil War, but he was assassinated in 1865 before Reconstruction truly began

absolute location

absolute monarchy

Adam Smith

a location identifiable by specific geographic coordinates

unrestricted rule by a king or queen

economic theorist who espoused capitalism

Algonquin

ancient Egyptians

anthropology

northeastern Native American civilization in the Great Lakes region

emerged as early as 5000 BCE in the Nile Valley; known for their pyramids, art, use of papyrus as paper, and pictorial writing (hieroglyphs); united under one monarch, or pharaoh

the study of humans and their cultures

Apartheid

arms race

Articles of Confederation

oppressive social system in South Africa that separated people by race in public places; led to structural inequalities and lowered standard of living for people of color; lasted for most of the twentieth century

competitive weapons development between the US and the USSR during the 1980s; the US intended to outspend the USSR, thereby weakening it

the original framework of the US government, designed to create a loose confederation between the colonies (now states) while allowing them to retain much of their individual sovereignty; created an intentionally weak, democratic government

assembly line

Assyria

Atahuallpa

a labor-intensive method of production developed by Henry Ford in which workers repetitively execute separate key tasks in production, expediting the product's completion

Sumerian-based civilization in the Near East; established military dominance and played an important role in regional trade

the last independent Inca emperor, defeated by Francisco Pizzaro in 1533

Athens

Augustus Caesar

Axis

ancient Greek city-state that became a revolutionary democracy controlled by the poor and working classes around 460 BCE; the first known democracy

Julius Caesar's nephew Octavian who gained control of Rome in 27 BCE and became the first Roman emperor

the alliance of Germany, Italy, and Japan during WWII

Aztecs

Babylonia

Barack Obama

militaristic Mesoamerican civilization that dominated Mexico and Central America before European contact

Sumerian-based civilization in Mesopotamia; developed courts and an early codified rule of law—the Code of Hammurabi—"an eye for an eye, a tooth for a tooth"

first African American president, elected in 2008; ended wars in Afghanistan and Iraq; halted the Great Recession; developed programs to provide healthcare to uninsured Americans

Bastille

Battle of Bunker Hill

Battle of Fort Sumter

Paris prison stormed on July 16, 1789 when the king sent troops to Paris; symbolic of tyranny

took place on June 17, 1775; caused King George III to declare that the colonies were in rebellion

1861 attack on Union troops in Sumter, South Carolina, by Confederate forces shortly after South Carolina seceded from the Union; this battle sparked the Civil War

Battle of Lexington and Concord

Battle of Tours (or Poitiers)

Battle of Yorktown

beginning of violent conflict between American rebel militiamen (minutemen) and the British in 1775

victory by Charles Martel in 732 CE that stopped Islamic incursions into Europe

1781 defeat of British forces by the Continental Army with support from France, ending the Revolutionary War

Berlin Conference

Bill of Rights

Boston Massacre

1884 conference in Berlin where Africa was divided up into colonies controlled by European powers as part of the *scramble for Africa*, without regard for Africans

the first ten amendments to the US Constitution; a set of guarantees of certain rights enjoyed by Americans

1770 event in which British troops fired on a crowd of American protestors

Boston Tea Party

bourgeoisie (communism and socialism)

bourgeoisie (French Revolution)

1773 protest of the Tea Act in which American colonial protestors disguised as Native Americans tossed tea off a ship in Boston Harbor

the class that owns the means of production and profits from the labor of the workers (proletariat); in communism, the proletariat are encouraged to overthrow the bourgeoisie

in eighteenth-century France, the emergent middle class growing powerful thanks to early capitalism, but not traditionally nobles or landowners under the feudal system; along with peasants, bore the brunt of taxation

Bubonic (Black) Plague

capitalism

cardinal directions

bacterial infection with global effects that killed a third of Europeans in the fourteenth century; led to broader social change

the *laissez-faire* (or free market) theory of economics in which government should not interfere with trade; problems in the market like monopolies would lead to inefficiencies and thus correct themselves

north, south, east, and west

Cesar Chavez

Charlemagne

Charles Martel

civil rights activist; led the United Farm Workers, who advocated for Hispanic farm workers who faced racial discrimination, poor treatment, and low pay

Frankish (French) leader who united much of Western Europe in the Middle Ages following chaotic period after the fall of the Roman Empire, leading to more organization and strengthening of the feudal system; crowned emperor in 800 CE

Frankish (French) leader who stopped Islamic incursions into Europe from Iberia (al Andalus)

checks and balances

Cherokee

Christopher Columbus

each branch of government has certain powers that limit the power of the other branches

Southeastern Native American civilization thought to be descended from the Iroquois; emerged in present-day Georgia; forced during the Trail of Tears to leave their land and migrate to Indian Territory (Oklahoma)

explorer who arrived in the Americas while seeking a sea route west from Europe to Asia

Church of England

Civil Rights Movement

Cold War

Protestant church founded by King Henry VIII; after years of conflict, would become the dominant religion in England

social and political movement for the rights of African Americans and other disenfranchised people in the 1960s

period of ongoing tension and conflict between the US and the USSR, the post-WWII global superpowers; remained "cold" because the two countries never engaged in direct military confrontation

Columbian Exchange

Committees of Correspondence

communism

describes the broad exchange of people, ideas, organisms, and technology across the Atlantic (encompassing *triangular trade*)

colonial rebel protest group that distributed anti-British propaganda

Marxist theory that revolution (class war) is needed to achieve a socialist society

Communist Manifesto

concentration camps

conflict

nineteenth-century pamphlet written by Marx and Engels about socialism; called for revolution against the capitalist system; inspired the formation of socialist groups worldwide

forced labor and death camps where the Nazis imprisoned and killed Jews, Roma, Slavic people, homosexuals, disabled people, people of color, prisoners of war, communists, and others as part of the Holocaust

the process of disagreement, usually resolved when one of the parties receives either the entirety or a satisfactory amount of the desired goal

Congress

Congress of Vienna

Constitution

the branch of the federal government that makes laws (the legislative branch); technically, it has the most power in government

following defeat of Napoleon in 1815, the conference where Prussia, the Austro-Hungarian Empire, Russia, and Britain agreed on balance of power in Europe; the first real international peace conference; set the precedent for European political organization

the document that provides the framework for the US government

Constitutional Convention

cooperation

Counter-Reformation

1787 meeting of the states to resolve problems arising from limitations on federal power. A decision was made to completely throw out the old Articles and write a new governing document from scratch—the Constitution

the process of working together to achieve similar goals; often leads to positive outcomes

attempts at reinforcing Catholic dominance throughout Europe during and after the Reformation in the wake of the Renaissance and related social change

Creek, Chickasaw, and Choctaw

Crusade

cuneiform

major Muskogean-speaking southeastern Native American civilizations; descendants of the Mississippi Mound Builders

holy war launched by Christian Europeans against Muslims in the Holy Land following decline of Christian Byzantine Empire; several crusades occurred for varying political reasons

a Sumerian development; the earliest known example of writing using characters to form words (not pictographs)

D-Day

Declaration of Independence

Declaration of the Rights of Man and the Citizen

June 6, 1944, when the US led the invasion of Normandy, invading Europe during WWII

issued on July 4, 1776, this document, written in great part by Thomas Jefferson and signed by the leaders of the Second Continental Congress, asserted US independence from Britain

precursor to the revolutionary French constitution assuring liberty and equality; written in the model of Enlightenment thought

demand

demokratia

desert

how much desire there is for a product or service

ancient Greek word meaning "people power"

a climate located in the low latitudes north and south of the savannah; the hottest and driest parts of the earth; receives less than 10 inches of rainfall a year

East African slave trade

economic regulation

Elizabeth Cady Stanton

Arabs, Asians and other Africans kidnapped African people and enslaved them throughout the Arab world and South Asia; later, Europeans did the same in African, Asian, and Indian Ocean colonies

indirect or direct price control by the government

women's rights activist; founded the National Woman Suffrage Association and led the 1848 Seneca Falls Convention on women's rights

Emancipation Proclamation

encomienda

English Bill of Rights

January 1, 1863 declaration by President Lincoln abolishing slavery in the US rebel states

Spanish political and economic system in which the king granted European landowners the "right" to hold lands in the Americas and demand labor and tribute from the local inhabitants

established constitutional monarchy in England in 1689

English Civil War

Enlightenment

Estates-General

1642 conflict between the Royalists, who supported the monarchy, and the Parliamentarians, who wanted a republic

the basis for reinvigorated European culture and political thought beginning around the eighteenth century that would drive its development

the weak representative governing assembly under the French king; included the clergy, the nobility, and the Third Estate (the middle class and the poor peasants); convened in an unsuccessful effort to resolve fiscal crisis prior to the outbreak of the French Revolution

euro

European Union

exchange

a common currency shared by some European countries

a forum for European countries to organize and cooperate politically, militarily, and economically; formed after the Cold War to promote European unity

the process of giving one thing and receiving another (usually with similar value) in return

feudalism

fiefs

First Continental Congress

socio-economic organization in medieval Europe; a hierarchy where land and protection were offered in exchange for loyalty

territory granted by lords to their vassals in exchange for loyalty under the feudal system

meeting of colonial leaders in Philadelphia in 1774, organized in response to the Intolerable Acts; colonial leaders later presented concerns to the king and were rebuffed

First Crusade

Forbidden City

Four Freedoms

invasion of the Holy Land and capture of Jerusalem by European Christians in 1099 in an effort to take the region from Islamic control

imposing home of the Chinese emperor; constructed under the Ming dynasty

in the context of the rise of fascism, FDR defined these as freedom of speech, freedom of religion, freedom from want, and freedom from fear

Francisco Pizzaro

Franco-Prussian War

Franklin Delano Roosevelt

Spanish conquistador who defeated the Inca king Atahuallpa, effectively beginning Spanish rule in the Andean region

1870 conflict when Prussia began to assert its military power and took control of mineral-rich Alsace-Lorraine from France; outcome helped fuel Prussian industrial development

elected to the presidency in 1932; developed the New Deal, rescuing the United States from the Great Depression, and led the country through WWII

Friedrich Engels

Genghis Khan

genocide

nineteenth-century German economist and philosopher who, with Karl Marx, developed socialism

Mongol leader who led expansion of the Mongol Empire in the twelfth and thirteenth centuries

killing people based on their ethnicity

geographic features

George Washington

glasnost

physical features of place like continents, bodies of water, plains, plateaus, mountains, and valleys

colonial military leader, general of the Continental Army, first US president; his able military leadership helped the colonies eventually secure independence, and his political leadership helped keep the young country united

Soviet reform meaning "openness"

government regulation

Great Depression

Great Fear

government involvement in the economy to effect an economic or social outcome

the global economic collapse that resulted in widespread poverty and unemployment in the United States and the world

terror among French peasants in 1789 over food shortages and a suspected conspiracy against the Third Estate

guillotine

Hapsburg Dynasty

Hernan Cortés

device used by the republican government to execute counter-revolutionaries in post-revolutionary France; symbolic of chaotic period during the Reign of Terror

powerful Catholic European ruling family that controlled Austria and Spain throughout Thirty Years' War and beyond

Spanish explorer who captured Aztec ruler Montezuma II and invaded Mexico

hieroglyphs

high latitudes

Holocaust

ancient Egyptian writing (unlike cuneiform, pictographs, or pictorial writing)

latitudes from 66.5° north and south to the poles

the dispossession, imprisonment, and murder of at least six million Jews, Roma, Slavic people, homosexuals, disabled people, people of color, prisoners of war, communists, and others by the Nazis

Holy Land

Holy Roman Empire

House of Representatives
(the lower house of Congress)

term to describe the Levant, location of holy cities and sites important to the three major monotheistic religions (Judaism, Christianity, and Islam); often used in reference to the Crusades

collection of disparate Germanic lands in Central Europe from 962 CE to 1806

the body of lawmakers in Congress with proportional representation reflecting the population of each state

human geography

humanism

humid continental climate

the study of the impact of people on the physical world

a mode of thought emphasizing human nature, creativity, and an overarching concept of truth; emerged during the European Renaissance

located in the middle latitudes, the agriculturally productive, true four-season climate

humid subtropical climate

Hundred Years' War

imperialism

located in the middle latitudes, a warm and moist climate on coastal areas north and south of the tropics that receive warm ocean currents and warm winds year round

ongoing conflict in Europe during the fourteenth and fifteenth century, particularly between England and France; period of political disorganization

the possession and exploitation of land overseas

Incas

Indian Removal Act

indulgences

Andean civilization dominant in western South America before European contact; constructed mountain transportation and agricultural infrastructure

1830 law that forced Cherokee, Creek, Chickasaw, Choctaw, and others from their lands in the Southeast to Indian Territory (Oklahoma)

promises that knights who fought in the Crusades would be forgiven for any sins committed and go to heaven

Industrial Revolution

industrialization

institutions

nineteenth-century economic revolution beginning in Europe marked by mechanization in agriculture and transportation and the emergence of factories

the process of manufacturing; the process of an economy transforming from dependence on agricultural to industrial production; replacement of hand labor by machines as the main way of manufacturing, exponentially increasing production capacities

extensions of core social values created in response to varying individual and group needs; include government, private enterprise, religious institutions, academic institutions, local communities, and the family unit

intermediate directions

Intolerable Acts

iron curtain

the directions between the cardinal directions

1774 Acts enforced by Britain in response to tensions and violence in the colonies, including closing Boston Harbor and bringing Massachusetts back under direct royal control

a metaphor for the concept of a post-WWII Europe divided between east (with communist governments generally aligned with the USSR) and west (with democratic capitalist governments generally aligned with the US)

Iroquois

Ivan the Great

Ivan the Terrible

northeastern Native American civilization in New York and southern Ontario/Quebec; a confederation of six tribes

Russian leader and monarch who defeated the Mongols to return Moscow and Slavic lands to Russian control in 1480; consolidated early Russian Empire

Russian monarch who expanded Russian territory into Europe; strengthened government and Russian Orthodox Christianity

Joan of Arc

John Adams

John Locke

French leader in the 1429 Battle of Orléans; inspired French resistance to English incursions

colonial leader, member of the Continental Congress, federalist, second US president, brother to the radical Samuel Adams; Adams supported a strong federal government and expanded executive power

Enlightenment thinker who believed in the social contract in exchange for protection and to enjoy social benefits, people relinquish some sovereignty to a republican government; influenced the American Revolution

Julius Caesar

Karl Marx

King Henry VIII

a popular Roman military leader who forced the corrupt Senate to give him control and who began transitioning Rome from a republic to what would become an empire; assassinated in 44 BCE

nineteenth-century German economist and philosopher who, with Friedrich Engels, developed socialism

sixteenth-century English monarch; rejected Catholicism; founder of the Church of England

King Louis XIV

Kingdom of Ghana

knights

seventeenth-century French monarch who consolidated the monarchy and disempowered the nobility; known as *the Sun King*

gold-rich kingdom in West Africa; important trading partner of North African Muslims on the Trans-Saharan trade routes

warriors who fought for lords; were usually rewarded with land and often became lords themselves

League of Nations

Leon Trotsky

Louisiana Purchase

a largely toothless international organization established after WWI and designed to prevent future outbreaks of international war; the basis for the later United Nations

revolutionary Russian socialist; ally of Lenin; a founder of the Soviet Union and leader of the Russian Revolution

1803 purchase of French-controlled territory in North America by the United States, authorized, controversially, by President Jefferson; nearly doubled the size of the country

low latitudes

Machu Picchu

Magna Carta

the region located from the equator to latitudes 23.5° north and south

Inca citadel in the Andes

English document that protected the property and rights of individuals; the basis for today's parliamentary system in that country; early version of a constitution

Malcolm X

Mali Empire

Manifest Destiny

civil rights leader who championed better living standards for blacks in northern cities and the empowerment of African American communities

powerful African Islamic empire based at Timbuktu; rich in salt and gold

the concept that it was the mission and fate of the United States to expand westward and settle the continent

Mansa Musa

Marie Antoinette

marine climate

emperor of the Mali Empire; made pilgrimage to Mecca in 1324, showing influence of the empire

unpopular French queen during the French Revolution; symbolic of the nobility's disconnection with and abuse of the people; came under suspicion for her Austrian origins; ultimately arrested and assassinated

the warm and rainy climate located in the middle latitudes in areas that are near or surrounded by water

maroon communities

Martin Luther

Martin Luther King, Jr.

settlements of escaped slaves in the Western Hemisphere

Catholic monk who wrote a letter of protest to the pope in 1517 known as the Ninety-Five Theses

civil rights leader who fought for equal rights for African Americans; embraced peaceful protest as a means to achieve legislative and social change to end segregation between black and white Americans

Marxism-Leninism

mass production

Maya

revolutionary concept of socialism developed by Vladimir Lenin and inspiration for the Soviet Union

large-scale production of consumer products (enabled by the assembly line and factories)

dominated the Yucatan peninsula around 300 CE; had a complex spiritual belief system; detailed calendar, written language, and pyramidal temples; studied astronomy and mathematics

Mecca

Mediterranean climate

Mehmed the Conqueror

birthplace of Muhammad; holy city of Islam

a climate located in the middle latitudes between latitudes 30° and 40° north and south characterized by wet, mild winters and dry, warm summers

fifteenth-century Ottoman caliph who expanded the empire from Hungary through Mesopotamia

Meiji Restoration

mercantilism

Middle Ages

period of technological and military modernization in Japan beginning in 1868; helped Japan become an important military power

economic system in which the colonizing country took raw materials from colonies for its own benefit, amassing wealth through protectionism and increasing exports at the expense of other rising colonial powers

time period from the fall of Rome to around the tenth century in Europe

middle latitudes

migration

Ming Dynasty

the region located from latitudes 23.5°to 66.5° north and south

patterns of movement from one place to another, with the intention of settling permanently at the new location

reestablished ethnic Han Chinese control in fourteenth-century China following the Yuan period; oversaw expansion of Chinese power; fostered cultural development

Missouri Compromise

Mongol Empire

monopoly

1820 legislation that allowed Missouri to join the union as a slave state but provided that any other states north of the thirty-sixth parallel (36°30') would be free

Central Asian empire that dominated most of Eurasia thanks to the Mongols' equestrian and archery skills and lack of a dominant regional power

the control of a market for a good or service by one company or group

Montesquieu

Montezuma II

Moors

French Enlightenment thinker who introduced the idea of the separation of powers, an important element of the American democracy

Aztec leader when Europeans arrived in Mesoamerica; captured by Spanish explorer Hernan Cortés

North African Muslims who invaded and settled Iberia (al Andalus)

Mughal Empire

Muhammad

multinational corporations (MNCs)

composed of small kingdoms in Indian Subcontinent from the sixteenth century until British rule; influential in Indian Ocean trade routes

Arab leader who introduced Islam and lead conquest of Arabian Peninsula

companies based in one country with operations in one or more other countries; the primary driving forces of globalization

Napoleon Bonaparte

Napoleonic Wars

nation-state

nineteenth-century French emperor who conquered much of Europe, changing political balance of power on the continent

series of early–nineteenth-century wars between Napoleonic France and various European powers; ultimately resulting in new balance of power in Europe

sovereign territory ruled by an ethnic majority

nationalism

natural resources

Navajo

sentiment of loyalty to one's own cultural or ethnic group above others; premise for independence movements among ethnic groups under imperial control in Europe during Age of Revolutions

---

fresh water, arable land, fuel, livestock, and game

---

a pastoral people that controlled territory in present-day Arizona, New Mexico, and Utah; descendants of the Ancestral Pueblo or Anasazi, who built cliff dwellings

New Deal

Nile Valley

Ninety-Five Theses

plan presented by FDR to rescue the United States from the Great Depression; included emergency acts to save the banking system and long-term relief for the poor and unemployed

the fertile land on the banks of the Nile River conducive to agriculture and irrigation

letter of protest written in 1517 to the pope by the monk Martin Luther; expressed dissatisfaction with the state of the Catholic Church; ideas at the heart of the Protestant Reformation

nuclear weapons

opportunity cost

Otto von Bismarck

very powerful weapons that can destroy entire cities; possessed by only a few world powers; first developed by the United States and the Soviet Union

when a consumer makes a choice at the cost of another choice or the value of an opportunity

Prussian leader who consolidated the linguistically and culturally Germanic, Central European states of Prussia into the German Empire in 1871

Ottoman Empire

Pax Romana

Pearl Harbor

Turkic empire that controlled Anatolia, the Balkans, and eventually the Middle East and much of the Mediterranean world; Ottomans captured Istanbul, capital of the Ottoman Empire, in 1453

a period of stability in the Mediterranean region under the Roman Empire

US military base in Hawaii; on December 7, 1941, Japan attacked Pearl Harbor, causing the US to enter WWII

perestroika

pharaoh

physical geography

a term meaning "transparency" referring to Soviet reform

ancient Egyptian monarch

the study of the natural processes of the earth

Plains tribes

polis

political features

included the Sioux, Cheyenne, Apache, Comanche, and Arapaho who lived in the Great Plains area; nomadic peoples; depended mainly on the buffalo for sustenance

ancient Greek word meaning "city-state" or "community"

towns and cities; county, state, or national borders

pope

president

primary socialization

the leader of the Catholic Church; in medieval Europe, also a powerful political leader

the head of state and head of the executive branch; has the power to appoint federal officials and judges, sign or veto laws (approve or deny them), and make foreign policy; he or she is also the commander-in-chief of the US armed forces

when a child learns the values, actions, and attitudes that are appropriate for members of his or her particular culture

printing press

pyramids

Quartering Act

device enabled the rapid production and distribution of written manuscripts, thereby spreading information more widely

Egyptian burial tombs for pharaohs

a 1765 law that forced American colonists to provide shelter, even in their homes, to British troops stationed in the region

Queen Victoria

Qur'an

Reconquista

eighteenth-century British monarch who oversaw imperial expansion throughout India, Australia, and large parts of Africa

the holy book of Islam

Christian raids of Islamic Spain (al-Andalus); expulsion of Islamic powers from Iberia; and unification of Christian kingdoms in Spain into one Christian kingdom

Reformation

regions

relative location

movement for reform of the Catholic Church; resulted in new factions of Christianity in Europe

parts of the world with definable and identifiable characteristics

where a place is situated in relation to another place or places

Renaissance

reparations

Rousseau

revival of learning, art, architecture, and philosophy in Europe, especially influenced by work from ancient Greece and Rome; triggered social change and backlash against the church

costly financial compensation charged of Germany by the victors of WWI to cover the cost of the war

French Enlightenment thinker who believed in the social contract and the concept of the rule of law, which would bring stability to a republic founded on the social contract; influenced the American and French Revolutions

Russo-Japanese War

Samuel Adams

savannah

1905 defeat of Russia by Japan that cemented Japan's status as an emerging industrial and military world power; signaled decline of imperial Russia

radical colonial American rebel; leader of the Sons and Daughters of Liberty and Committees of Correspondence

climate located in the low latitudes north and south of the rainforest; dry in the winter and wet in the summer, experiencing an average of 10 to 30 inches of rain

scarcity

Scientific Revolution

Scramble for Africa

insufficient supply to meet demand

time of scientific exploration and discoveries based in Islamic and ancient Greek and Roman scholarship; threatened the power of the Catholic Church

term used to describe rapid nineteenth-century European colonization of Africa; African colonization symbolized power and prestige among European countries

Second Continental Congress

Second Industrial Revolution

secondary socialization

meeting of colonial leaders in Philadelphia in 1775 when colonial leaders agreed on declaring independence and forming the United States of America

occurred in the late nineteenth and early twentieth century; based on heavy industry, railroads, and weapons

occurs when an individual learns the appropriate values, actions, attitudes, and behaviors as a member of a smaller group within a larger society

Senate

separation of powers

September 11, 2001

the body of lawmakers in Congress with equal representation—two senators are elected to represent each state (the upper house of Congress); governing body of republican ancient Rome as of 509 BCE

limits the powers within the federal government by dividing power among three branches

the executive, the legislative, and the judicial

the date that the United States was attacked by terrorists, resulting in thousands of civilian casualties and major land wars in Afghanistan and Iraq

serfs

Seven Years' War

Shawnee

peasants who remained on fiefs ("tied to the land") under feudalism; farmed for lords and granted small plots of land for personal use; were entitled to the lords' protection but not obligated to fight; not slaves, but not truly free persons

first true global conflict (1756 – 1763); conflict among Europeans over control of Hapsburg territories; conflict between England and France in North America and Asia for colonial power

an Algonquin-speaking people based in the Ohio Valley; Shawnee leader Tecumseh led the Northwest Confederacy against the United States in 1812

Silk Road

Simón Bolivar

social regulation

term to describe trade routes stretching from Europe to China through Central Asia; spurred global exchange of goods and information

nineteenth-century revolutionary Latin American leader

government regulation that encourages businesses to behave responsibly and prohibits harmful behavior

social structures

socialism

socialization

(as relates to geography) the organization of a society and how social events relate to and affect places, etc.

philosophy that workers (proletariat) should own the means of production and directly benefit from profits of their labor rather than the bourgeoisie, who could not be trusted to put the interests of the proletariat over profit

a process whereby individuals learn skills, beliefs, values, and behavior patterns of society and how these can influence their own norms and customs

sociology

Songhai Empire

Sons and Daughters of Liberty

the study of groups, institutions, and society

west-central African empire; succeeded the Mali Empire; rich in salt

colonial rebel protest group that carried out violent acts against tax collectors

Sparta

spatial relationships

Stamp Act

ancient Greek military city-state

how one place is located in relation to another place

controversial 1765 tax on all published documentation in the colonies; the first direct tax on the colonists

steam engine

steppes or prairie

suburbanization

important machine for Industrial Revolution; powered factories allowing them to be built anywhere

a climate located in the middle latitudes far from the ocean, characterized by flatlands and minimal rainfall

the movement of urban dwellers from cities to live in growing suburbs, semi-rural areas at the outskirts of cities

Suleiman the Magnificent

Sumerians

supply

sixteenth-century Ottoman caliph who consolidated Ottoman rule throughout the Mediterranean world

ancient Near Eastern people who emerged around 2500 BCE; developed irrigation, agriculture, education, math, astronomy, religion, art and literature, city-states, governance, and administration

how much of a product the market can actually offer

Susan B. Anthony

system of alliances

taiga

women's rights activist and leader in women's suffrage movement; leader at 1848 Seneca Falls Convention

the complicated diplomatic and military alliances among European powers that led to the outbreak and magnitude of WWI

a cold climate located in the high latitudes south of the tundra; contains the world's largest forestlands, extreme mineral wealth, and many swamps and marshes

taxes

Tea Act

Tenochtitlan

money paid by the people, organizations, and companies to the government. This money covers government expenses like federal employee salaries and retirement programs, government programs, and the military. It also helps fuel the economy

controversial 1773 tax on colonial tea that triggered the Boston Tea Party

capital of Aztec Empire near modern Mexico City

Third Estate

Thirty Years' War

Thomas Jefferson

the middle class (bourgeoisie) and peasants (commoners) of pre-revolutionary France; those who bore the brunt of taxation

European conflict (1618 – 1648) based on rifts between Protestant and Catholic Christianities and related alliances; outcome reinforced concept of state sovereignty in Europe

colonial leader, architect of the Declaration of Independence; third US president; Jefferson was antifederalist and disapproved of a strong US Constitution

tithe

Toussaint L'Ouverture

Trail of Tears

percentage of earnings (10 percent) owed as taxes to the nobility by peasants in pre-revolutionary France

leader of slave rebellion in Haiti, ultimately winning Haitian independence from France in 1791

the forced migration of Cherokee and others from their land in the Southeast to Indian Territory (today, Oklahoma) to make way for white settlers following the Indian Removal Act; the term describes the suffering, poor conditions, and death suffered by many during the migration

Treaty of Versailles

Treaty of Westphalia

trench warfare

316 Cirrus Test Prep | **Praxis II Elementary Education**

the treaty that ended WWI, held Germany accountable for the entirety of the war, and brought economic hardship to the country by forcing it to pay reparations to the other powers

ended the Thirty Years' War in 1648; established the concept of state sovereignty and non-interference; considered the foundation of modern international relations

bloody, long-term fighting in fortified trenches on the Western Front during WWI

triangular trade

Triple Alliance

tropical rainforests

pattern of trade in the Atlantic world

Europeans purchased or kidnapped Africans in West Africa to be enslaved, taken to the Americas, and traded for raw materials like sugar; these materials were taken to Europe and traded for consumer goods; and these goods were exchanged in Africa for slaves (and sometimes also in the colonies)

alliance of Austria-Hungary, Germany, and Italy in the First World War (against Russia, the United Kingdom, and France, the *Triple Entente*)

moist forests exhibiting high biodiversity, located mainly in the equatorial lowlands in Central Africa, Southeast Asia, and the Amazon basin

tundra

Underground Railroad

United Nations

a cold climate located in the high latitudes north of the taiga; with extremely cold and long winters, the ground is frozen for most of the year and becomes mushy during the short summer

a secret network of safe houses and connections to help Southern slaves escape to the North and to Canada

an international organization formed after WWII to prevent another world war, to champion human rights, and to uphold international security

urban planning

urbanization

vassals

managing the development and use of cities

the development of cities; became a feature of human development at the advent of the nineteenth-century Industrial Revolution, when unskilled jobs in factories attracted rural workers to cities, offering them higher wages than an agricultural lifestyle did

swore loyalty (fealty) to lords under the feudal system; were rewarded with land; shared yield

vice president

Vikings

Vladimir Lenin

fulfills the duties of the president when he or she is unable; becomes president in the event of the president's death; also serves as president of the Senate

Scandinavian seafaring civilization that explored the North Atlantic and northern Europe; evidence indicates the Vikings traveled as far as the eastern Mediterranean

revolutionary Russian socialist; believed in the *dictatorship of the proletariat*, or that socialism could not be maintained democratically; developed Marxism-Leninism; led the Russian Revolution; founder of the Soviet Union

Voltaire

War of 1812

white man's burden

French Enlightenment thinker critical of absolute monarchy, the Catholic Church, and censorship; influenced the French Revolution

conflict between the US, Britain, and the British-allied Northwest Confederacy (led by the Shawnee leader Tecumseh). The US maintained its territorial integrity despite British incursions from Canada; meanwhile, the US gained power in the Northwest (present-day Ohio Valley region), facilitating westward expansion despite resistance from the Shawnee and other tribes allied with the Confederacy

concept that drove nineteenth-century European imperialism; idea that white Europeans were justified in oppressing other peoples to "improve" them as European culture was "superior"

William the Conqueror

Yuan Dynasty

Norman leader who invaded England in 1066, bringing more organization and feudal economy

Mongol dynasty in China; upended local hierarchy, but maintained some traditional administrative and other functions

Science

acceleration

acid

how quickly an object changes velocity

a compound that is able to contribute a hydrogen ion and has a pH lower than 7

ALTO– cloud

amphibians

amplitude

a cloud located in the middle level of the sky

a class of cold-blooded vertebrate animals that have gills when they hatch but develop lungs in adulthood

a measure of a wave's displacement from its rest position

anatomy

Animalia

anther

the study of the structure of living organisms

the kingdom that contains multicellular organisms that can move around and must consume other organisms for energy

part of the male reproductive organ of a flowering plant where pollen is stored

antibodies

antigens

artery

special proteins that bind to foreign substances in the body and neutralize them

substances that the body recognizes as foreign

a blood vessel that carries blood away from the heart

asexual

asthenosphere

asteroid

does not require the union of sex cells to reproduce

the hot, semisolid part of the mantle under the lithosphere

a large rocky body, smaller than a planet, that orbits the sun

atmosphere

atom

atomic mass

the mass of gases that surround Earth

the smallest particle of a chemical element that retains the properties of the element

the mass of an atom calculated by adding the number of protons and neutrons

atomic number

attraction

B cells

the number of protons in the nucleus of an atom

a force that draws objects closer

(also called B lymphocytes) produce special proteins called antibodies that bind to foreign substances, called antigens, and neutralize them

balanced equation

base

biofuel

a chemical equation where the same amount of each element is represented on both side (the reactants and the products have equal amounts of each element)

a compound that is able to contribute a hydroxide ion and has a pH greater than 7

biological matter that can be burned to produce heat, steam, or electricity

biomass

biomes

birds

plant-based fuel, usually burned, for generating heat, steam, or electricity

large geographic areas that provide the environmental conditions in which certain organisms live

endothermic vertebrate animals that have wings, feathers, scaly legs, beaks, and no teeth, and bear their young in a hard-shelled egg

black holes

calyx

capillaries

a massive star that has collapsed and has a gravitational force so strong that light cannot escape

all of the sepals of a flower together

the smallest blood vessels in the body where gas exchange occurs

carbohydrates

carpel

cell

the sugars that act as a source of energy for all living things

the ovary of a flowering plant where the ova are produced

the smallest living part of an organism

cell division

cell membrane

cell wall

the separation of a cell into two cells with identical genes

the outer covering of a cell

hard outer structure of a plant cell

cellular metabolism

cerebellum

cerebrum

(also called cellular respiration) how cells produce energy

part of the brain located at the back and bottom that controls motor movements

the biggest part of the brain, the wrinkly gray part at the front and top, that controls different body functions like thinking, vision, hearing, touch, and smell

cervix

chemical change

chlorophyll

the passage that connects the uterus to the vagina

making or breaking chemical bonds between atoms in a chemical reaction

a chemical in the leaves of plants that uses energy from sunlight to convert water and carbon dioxide into sugars

chromosome

cinder cone volcano

cirrus cloud

dense strands of DNA that contain the genetic code of an organism

a small, steep volcano formed by ash with a single lava vent and a crater on top

a thin, wispy cloud that appears high in the sky

classification

climate

climate zone

sorting according to characteristics

an area's weather conditions over time

a large area that experiences similar average temperature and precipitation

cloud

color

combustion

billions of tiny water droplets floating in the air together

frequency of a light wave

a chemical reaction that produces carbon dioxide and water, usually from the burning of fuels

comet

communities

competition

a small object made of ice and dust that orbits the sun

interdependent organisms living together in a habitat

occurs when two organisms needs to use the same resources

composite volcano

compound

conclusions

a cone-shaped volcano with steep sides made of lava, ash, and rock

a combination of two or more elements

inferences based on data collected in an experiment

condensation

conduction

conductivity

the process by which water vapor in the air turns into liquid water when it comes into contact with a cold surface

the transfer of heat through physical contact

a property that determines how well a material conducts electricity and heat

conifers

conservation

continent

nonflowering plants that produce seeds protected by woody cones

protecting the environment and natural resources

one of seven large land masses on Earth's surface

continental drift

control group

convection

slow movement of Earth's tectonic plates

the parts of an experiment that stay the same

transfer of heat that occurs in a circular motion caused by heat rising and cold sinking

convergent plate boundary

coral reef

core

when two tectonic plates crash into one another

a marine (saltwater) system with high levels of diversity

the layer at the center of the earth

corolla

cotyledon

covalent bond

all of the petals of a flower together

plant embryo inside a seed

a chemical bond in which electrons are shared

crust

cumulus cloud

current

thin and broken outermost surface layer of the earth

tall, puffy clouds that are often dark at the bottom and whiter toward the top

the movement of electrons through a circuit

currents

decomposer

decomposition

movements of ocean water caused by differences in salt content or temperature and winds

organism that breaks down dead matter

a chemical reaction in which a single substance is broken down into two or more substances

density

dependent variable

deposition

a property of matter that can be determined by dividing mass by volume

part of an experiment that responds to, or depends on, the independent variable

the laying down of sediment in a new location

desert

dicot

displacement

a biome with extreme temperatures and very low rainfall with specialized vegetation and small mammals

a seed with two cotyledons

a measure of the shortest distance between the initial and final locations of a moving point

divergent plate boundary

DNA

dominant

a boundary between two tectonic plates that are moving away from one another

deoxyribonucleic acid (carries genetic information)

genetic traits that are expressed as characteristics of an organism

Doppler effect

drainage basin

earthquake

the change in wavelength when waves are compressed as an object approaches an observer and spread out as the object moves away from the observer

a given area of land from which all rainfall flows into a single body of water

violent shaking of the ground caused by tectonic plates crashing into or scraping against each other

eclipse

ecological succession

ecology

when Earth, the moon, and the sun align so that light from one object is blocked

the process by which ecosystems change and develop over time

study of organisms' interactions with each other and the environment

ecosystem

ectotherm

electric charge

a community of organisms and their interaction with each other and the environment

a cold-blooded organism

a difference in the balance of protons and electrons that creates a positively or negatively charged object

electricity

electromagnetic waves

electron

energy of moving electrons

waves composed of oscillating electric and magnetic fields

subatomic particle with a negative charge found outside the nucleus of an atom

elements

endosperm

endotherm

substances made of one type of atom

part of a seed that provides nourishment for the plant embryo

a warm-blooded organism

endothermic

energy

enzyme

a chemical reaction that requires energy

the capacity of an object to do work

a special type of protein that can cause or speed up a specific chemical reaction

equilibrium

erosion

eukaryotic cells

a state of balance

the movement of sediments from one place to another

cells that contain a nucleus and are found in multicellular organisms

evaporation

evolution

exothermic

the process of changing from a liquid to a gas

the progressive changes of living things throughout Earth's history

a chemical reaction in which energy (heat) is released

experimental design

experimental error

fallopian tubes

an experiment that includes an objective, standard protocols, a control group, and independent and dependent variables

mistakes made during an experiment caused by limitations of the equipment or external influences

tubes that transfer eggs from the ovaries to the uterus in the female reproductive system

fertilization

filament

food web

joining of the male and female reproductive cells

a long stalk-like structure that supports a plant's anther

producers, consumers, predators, and decomposers that live interdependently in an ecosystem

force

fossil

fossil fuels

any push or pull on an object

preserved remains or traces of ancient life

nonrenewable fuels made from organisms that lived millions of years ago

frequency

friction

fruit

the number of times per second a wave cycles

the force of one object resisting another

provides protection and nourishment for the seeds of flowering plants

function

fungi

galaxy

the activity of a part of an organism

a group of unicellular and multicellular organisms that have cell walls and reproduction strategies that differ from those in the other kingdoms of life

a large system of stars, gas, and dust held together by gravity

gas

geology

geothermal

matter with widely dispersed molecules that can change both shape and volume

the study of Earth

converting heat from below the Earth's surface to make steam

germination

gene

generator

when a seed begins to grow

genetic code that determines the characteristics of an organism

a device that transforms mechanical energy into electrical energy

genetic

genetic disorder

genus

hereditary

a hereditary abnormality that creates a health condition

the level of taxonomic classification that ranks above species

geology

geothermal energy

germination

the study of Earth

converting heat from below Earth's surface to make steam

when a seed begins to grow

gestation

glacier

gravity

the development of an embryo in the uterus

a large mass of slowly moving ice and snow

the attraction of one mass to another mass

greenhouse gases

groundwater

gymnosperm

gases that trap heat in the atmosphere

water that is stored underground in rock layers called aquifers

a nonflowering plant that produces seeds

heart

heat

helper T cells

the organ that pumps blood throughout the body

movement of energy from one substance to another

coordinate production of antibodies by B cells and removal of infected cells by T cells

homeostasis

hormones

hurricane

regulation and stabilization of internal conditions

chemicals that regulate bodily processes

a large, violent storm with winds 74 mph or greater

hydrology

hydropower

hydrosphere

the study of water

transforms the energy of moving water into mechanical energy and then electricity

the water found on and below Earth's surface and in the atmosphere

hypothesis

iceberg

igneous rock

an educated guess

a large chunk of ice that has broken off from a continental glacier and is floating in the ocean

formed from magma brought to Earth's surface as a result of tectonic processes

independent variables

inheritance

insulators

part of an experiment that is manipulated to test the effect on the dependent variable

a feature passed down from one generation to the next

materials that do not conduct heat or electricity well

invertebrate

ionic bond

isotope

an organism that does not have a backbone

a chemical bond that involves the attraction between two ions with unlike charges

a variation of an element with a different number of neutrons in its nucleus

keystone species

killer T cells

kinetic energy

a species whose removal decreases the overall diversity of the ecosystem

destroy infected body cells after they are identified and removed by T cells

the energy of motion

kingdom

lake

laws

the highest level of taxonomic classification

inland body of fresh water

descriptions of scientific phenomena

leaves

lens

life cycle

the part of a plant where photosynthesis takes place

curved piece of glass that can be used to bend light

the stages of life of an organism

lipids

liquid

lithosphere

organic molecule used for energy storage and other cellular functions

matter with more loosely packed molecules that can change shape but not volume

the outer layer of the earth that includes the crust and upper layer of the mantle

loudness

lunar eclipse

magma

the amplitude of a sound wave

when Earth lines up between the moon and sun; the moon moves into Earth's shadow and appears dark in color

melted rock

magnetic field lines

magnets

mammals

show the direction of a magnetic field at different points

materials that create a magnetic field

a class of warm-blooded vertebrate animals that have hair, give birth to live young (with a few exceptions), and produce milk

mantle

mass

matter

the layer of Earth below the crust

the amount of matter in an object

any substance that takes up space and has mass

measurement tools

medical technology

medicine

equipment used to collect data

research and development for improving patient care

pharmaceuticals used to treat or prevent medical conditions

medulla

meiosis

memory cells

(also called the brain stem) the part of the brain where it connects to the spinal cord and controls automatic body functions like breathing and heartbeat

formation of reproductive cells

remember antigens that have been removed so the immune system can respond more quickly if they enter the body again

metamorphic rock

meteorology

mineral

forms when extreme temperature and pressure cause the structure of preexisting rocks to change

the study of the atmosphere and weather

a naturally occurring, solid, inorganic substance with a crystalline structure

mitochondria

mitosis

mixture

cell organelle that produces energy in the form of ATP

process of cell division

two or more substances combined without a chemical reaction to bond them

models

molecule

monera

representations of the real world

two or more atoms bonded together

unicellular organisms that have no nucleus

monocot

moon

mutation

a seed with only one cotyledon

a large body that orbits a planet

a change in genetic information that may be passed on to future generations

natural selection

nervous system

neurons

Darwin's theory that living things that adapt to their environment have a higher survival rate and produce more offspring

processes external stimuli and sends signals throughout the body

cells that make up the peripheral nervous system and transmit information through electrical signals

neutralization

neutron

Newton's first law of motion

a chemical reaction that occurs when an acid and a base react to form a salt and water

subatomic particle with no charge found within the nucleus of an atom

an object at rest stays at rest, and an object in motion stays in motion, unless a force acts on it

Newton's second law of motion

Newton's third law of motion

nimbus cloud

force equals mass multiplied by acceleration; $F = ma$

for every action, there is an equal and opposite reaction

one that has a lot of water vapor in it and will most likely lead to precipitation

nonrenewable resources

nuclear power

nucleic acid

resources that take millions of years to replenish

energy stored in large atoms that is released when such atoms are broken into smaller atoms

linear biomolecules composed of nucleotide bases that store the genetic code of an organism

nucleus

ocean

optics

the center of a cell that contains DNA

large body of salt water

the study of light

organ

organ systems

organelle

a body part that serves an important function in a system

groups of organs that work together to perform one or more functions

part of a cell that is specialized to perform a specific function

organism

ova

ovaries

a living thing

(also called eggs) the female reproductive cells of a plant

organs which produce female gametes (eggs)

oxidation

ozone layer

paleontology

a chemical change in which a substance loses electrons

part of the stratosphere that captures harmful radiation from the sun

the study of the history of life through fossils

parasitism

penis

period

a relationship between two organisms when one organism benefits to the detriment of the other

organ of the male reproductive system through which sperm and urine pass out of the body

the time between wave crests

periodic table

petals

pH scale

a table of chemical elements listed in order by atomic number

special brightly colored leaves that form flowers

a standard measure of acidity or alkalinity where 7 is neutral

phase

phloem

photosynthesis

the position on a wave cycle at a given point in time

a special tissue that transports sugar and other nutrients throughout a plant

the process by which plants use energy from sunlight to make food (glucose) from carbon dioxide and water

physical change

physiology

pistil

change in a substance that does not change the composition of the substance

the study of the functions of living organisms

the female reproductive organ of a flowering plant

pitch

planet

plants

the frequency of vibrations

a large body in space that orbits a star

a kingdom of organisms that make food using photosynthesis

plasma

polar ice

poles

a state of matter similar to a gas that contains freely moving charged particles, although its charge remains neutral

large sheets of ice covering the North and South Poles

the ends of a magnet

pollen

population

potential energy

male reproductive cells of a plant

a group of organisms of the same species

the amount of energy of an object due to its position

precipitation

predators

prey

any form of water that falls from the sky

animals that kill other animals for food

an organism that is hunted and killed for food

primary consumer

primary succession

producer

animal that consumes plant matter (herbivore)

the development and changes that occur during colonization of a new habitat

an organism that produces energy directly from the sun

product

prokaryotic cells

property

new substance formed during a chemical reaction

cells that do not have a nucleus and are found in single-celled organisms like bacteria

a characteristic

prostate

proteins

protist

a muscular gland approximately the size of a walnut that is located between the male bladder and penis and produces a fluid that nourishes and protects sperm

chains of linked amino acids that perform a variety of biological functions

unicellular organisms with a nucleus

protons

Punnett square

radiation

subatomic particle with a positive electric charge found within the nucleus of an atom

a special chart that shows all of the possible genetic combinations from parents with given genotypes

transfer of heat without a medium

reactant

recessive

reflect

a substance that is changing in a chemical reaction

genetic traits that are not expressed as characteristics of an organism

change the direction of a light wave by bouncing the wave off a surface

refract

renewable resources

reproduction

bend a light wave as the wave travels through different media

resources that replenish quickly

the process of making a copy

reptiles

repulsion

ribosome

a class of cold-blooded vertebrates that have scales and lay eggs on land

a force that pushes objects away

cell organelle that produces proteins

river

rock

rock record

body of water that flows across the land as a result of rainfall, usually toward a lake, sea, or ocean

a naturally occurring organic or inorganic solid that is composed of one or more minerals

a biological history of Earth recorded in rocks

roots

scalar

sea

the part of a plant that absorbs water and nutrients from the soil

a measure of magnitude only

smaller body of salt water

secondary consumer

secondary succession

sedimentary rock

animal that consumes herbivores (carnivore)

changes to previously colonized habitats that have been disrupted

formed from the compaction of rock fragments that results from weathering and erosion

seed

sepals

sexual

plant embryo

special leaves that support the petals of a flower

requires the union of gametes (sex cells) to reproduce

shield volcano

solar eclipse

solar energy

a dome-shaped volcano with gently sloping sides made mostly of fluid lava flows

when the moon lines up between the earth and sun, blocking the sunlight

converts energy from the sun into electricity

solar system

solid

solubility

a system that includes a star or stars, along with planets, moons, asteroids, meteoroids, and comets, that is held together by gravity

matter with densely packed molecules that does not change volume or shape

the amount of a solute that will dissolve in a solvent

solute

solution

solvent

a substance being dissolved

a mixture that is evenly distributed and thoroughly dissolved

a substance in which another material is being dissolved

sound

species

speed

a longitudinal wave created by vibrations

the most specific level of taxonomic classification, in which organisms with similar genetics can breed

distance divided by time

spores

stamen

stars

526 Cirrus Test Prep | **Praxis II Elementary Education**

a single-celled reproductive body produced by some plants

male reproductive organ of a flowering plant where pollen is produced

large masses of gas

stem

stigma

stratus cloud

the main stalk of a plant that carries the nutrients and water from the roots to other parts of the plant

a female reproductive organ of a flowering plant where pollen is received

a flat, wispy cloud found in the lower level of the sky

stream

style

sun

smaller body of water that flows across the land as a result of rainfall, usually toward a river

an extended stalk that supports the stigma of a flowering plant

the star in Earth's solar system

synthesis

system

T cells

a chemical reaction in which two substances combine to form a single substance

a collection of interconnected parts that make up a complex whole with defined boundaries

(also called T lymphocytes) remove body cells that have been infected by foreign invaders like bacteria or viruses

tectonic plates

temperate broadleaf forest

temperate grassland

large plates that form the outer surface of the earth's crust and float on deeper liquid layers

a biome with moderate precipitation and temperatures with deciduous trees dominating

a biome with moderate precipitation and distinct seasons with grasses and shrubs dominating

temperature

tertiary consumer

testes

a measure of the kinetic energy of all the atoms or molecules in a substance, observed as how hot or cold the object is

carnivore that eats other carnivores

organs which produce male gametes (sperm)

theory

tides

tissue

principle explained by science

the movement of large bodies of water caused by the gravitational pull of the moon and the sun

groups of cells that have a similar function

tornado

traits

transform plate boundary

fast-moving, rotational winds that occur when unstable warm and cold air masses collide

characteristics

when two tectonic plates slide against each other in opposite directions

tropical rainforest

tundra

urethra

a hot and wet biome with an extremely high diversity of species

a biome with extremely low temperatures and short growing seasons with little or no tree growth

pass through which sperm passes

uterus

vacuole

vas deferens

organ in which embryos develop

cell organelle that **stores water and other molecules**

tube that carries sperm from the testes

vector

vein

velocity

a measure of both magnitude and direction

a blood vessel that carries blood to the heart from other parts of the body

the rate at which an object changes position; change of distance divided by change of time

vertebrate

volcanoes

water cycle

an organism that has a backbone

vents in Earth's crust that allow molten rock to reach the surface

the circulation of water throughout Earth's surface, atmosphere, and hydrosphere

watershed

wave

wave

a given area of land from which all rainfall flows into a single body of water

movement of energy through water

a pulse of energy

wavelength

weather

weathering

the distance between two points on back-to-back wave cycles

daily atmospheric conditions

the mechanical and/or chemical process by which rocks break down

weight

wind energy

xylem

the force of the gravitational pull on an object

energy from the wind is transformed into mechanical energy and then electricity

the special tissue that plants use to transport water and minerals

Made in the USA
Middletown, DE
15 March 2019